THE TRANSFORMATIONS OF GOD
SEVEN WOODCUTS BY ERNST BARLACH

with selections from his writings in translation by Naomi Jackson Groves

PRINTED IN GERMANY BY CHRISTIANS HAMBURG 1962

In any shape we know Thee
In any place we find Thee
Everywhere
Where Thou goest in the guise of Thine image
Thy creature modelled in clay

Though seeming transformed by the garbs of Time
Thy Being we always know

Ernst Barlach

The woodcuts that form the framework of this volume were cut by Ernst Barlach in Güstrow, Mecklenburg, in the years 1920–1921, from drawings made within the previous year or so. The collective title, »The Transformations of God – Die Wandlungen Gottes«, was given by the firm of Barlach's publisher, dealer, and friend, Paul Cassirer, then active in Berlin. Some of the titles by which the artist referred to individual woodcuts differ from those now generally used; »The Dance of Death«, for instance, he privately called »The Maligned Couple«, and »The Seventh Day« he originally named »Moses looking into the Promised Land«.

The arrangement as a set of seven, beginning with »The First Day« and ending with »The Seventh Day«, suggests the seven days of Creation but does not adhere to this theme in the central five subjects, which may be interpreted very generally as variations of the creative spirit at work in many forms. These seem to build up into a symmetrical pattern, with the Creator visible in solitary grandeur in the first two and the last two, while the three in central position may reveal his presence, not always visible, in complex relationship to mankind.

The presentation of a selection from Ernst Barlach's writings to accompany this cycle of prints is the fulfilment of a long-time wish. It is not an attempt to have the woodcuts ›illustrate‹ the words, nor to have the words ›explain‹ the woodcuts, but rather to show how the same artistic personality speaks first in one medium, then the other – and in Barlach's case this of course holds true for his sculpture as well, showing him to be probably the most striking example of the ›many-sided genius‹ in this rich century of ours.

The present selection makes no attempt to be fully representative of Barlach's total written œuvre, which includes eight plays, two novels and an autobiography as well as many short prose pieces and a few poems, the greater part already published during his lifetime (1870–1938), with the addition recently made available to the public of his richly revealing personal diary from the war years 1914–1917, as well as two volumes of his letters preserved by friends and relatives. Those who are acquainted with Ernst Barlach primarily as a sculptor – and this means most people who know his work, outside Germany at any rate – may be surprised at the quantity as well as the quality of his writing, which it is hoped will retain some of its pithy essence even in translation.

The present selection may be subjective rather than representative, however it is not a random choice but the assembling of passages in words that seem to show affinity in theme and mood with the seven woodcuts already presented as a cycle of ›Transformations‹.

In »The First Day« creative force seems to emerge in jagged flashes out of black chaos as the strong command rings forth: »Let there be Light!« The words selected as suitable for this Beginning reveal human intimations of divine intent, alongside man's consciousness of his own power to express what is within himself, searching outward, probing inward – God and Artist in creative counterpoint developing the themes of Transformation.

In »The Cathedrals« the spirit soars in contemplation of man's mighty symbols of God's glory, the towering medieval churches of Barlach's northern homeland. His words reveal his allegiance both to the past and to the modern Expressionist creed of spiritual regeneration which his friend, the poet-prophet Theodor Däubler, helped establish.

The third woodcut, »The Divine Beggar«, could serve as illustration to Barlach's play ›The Flood‹, published within a few years of the ›Transformations of God‹ as a fuller development of similar preoccupations. The theme of Suffering, central in this artist's philosophy as in that of many of his younger Expressionist contemporaries, is shown here in a strange and powerful way, with the patient Christ-like figure against a background of degraded humanity and what seems a torture-ladder descending from heaven to hell-on-earth. Suffering and responsibility, the mystic union of man with the universe, the destruction of one form to bring about renewal in another (which is of course the scientists' law of the conservation of matter) – are all woven into this phase of Transformation.

The title »Dance of Death« recalls medieval consciousness that in the midst of Life we are in Death. Serious intention seems to unite and impel the couple in Barlach's work (his »Maligned Couple«) as they shield themselves from Death and his comrades leering in the background. Passages from the plays and novels again reveal the double unity of Seen and Unseen as man faces thoughts of death and afterlife, and God's part in them.

Then, through the ghastly gluttony of »God Belly«, the speculating spirit may infer that Evil was created as a foil for Good, and that even in the face of mortal weakness the omnipresence of God may be sensed. The massive Moloch figure in the foreground of the woodcut can be interpreted in the obvious sense by Barlach's words concerning human greed and selfishness; the serious faces he has placed in the lower righthand corner (some are actual portraits of contemporary Expressionist writers) and the background figures of striding harpist and rapt visionary with arms upraised in prayer indicate a deeper level of the artist's consciousness of the complex counterpoint of Good and Evil in our day and our world.

»The Hills« lift up our eyes once more to heights of age-old grandeur, where God rests like a mighty fortress, the spirit contemplates and speculates upon the proofs and problems of creative labor.

Finally in »The Seventh Day« a warm sunset shimmer emanates from the Ancient of Days as he looks back philosophically upon Creation in all its phases. Here it seemed appropriate to select passages in words in which the aging artist, who constantly considered himself the modest transmitter of the Spirit, could likewise look back and »hold his own«.

It is hoped that this new combination of favorite themes will help to illuminate for English-speaking friends of Ernst Barlach some of the many facets of his creative mind, as well as demonstrate the unity within his manifold expression – providing, so to speak, brief glimpses through seven different windows into Ernst Barlach's house.

Ottawa, Canada, June 1962.   Naomi Jackson Groves

The Transformations of God are woodblock prints assembled around a central concept, and I should personally prefer not to put the interpretation of them into words. Experience shows that there is always one certain direction in which we can expend ourselves to the fullest degree, and in the Transformations I am a maker of woodcuts. However, a sentence or two may be of some use to you. Since my earliest days, and ever increasingly, I am conscious of the unity of Creator and Created. All that has come into being is simply the Creator in one form or another, his phases, his mirror-image; the Moment is simply a transformed fragment of Eternity.

Things change, evolve, dissolve, decay, then disappear into oblivion; but in all this process of change their Oneness is never lost. What happens at present will happen in another way in future, but the Power of Happening, the spirit of the Controlling Force, remains one and the same.

To be sure, these woodcuts are not in any sense the outcome of specially planned themes, nor did I assign myself the task of giving graphic formulation to any definite selection of mental concepts.

I beg you to be satisfied with these hints.

From a letter to Frau Frieda Strohm, dated Güstrow, February 8, 1931. Briefe II, 169.

Thou from everlasting unto everlasting

Thou Beginning without Ending

Thou Glory, Thou Holiness

Greatness, Goodness

Storm and Stillness

All-Seeming and All-Being

Dramen, 322

A storm comes up behind us, bows us forward, brings us trust. Not that we storm forward – we are being stormed. And the storm that gives direction to our feverish, stubborn will is nameless as primeval Power that pays no heed to our appeal, veritable as true Glory, real as God whom no one sees.

We feel this glory as we can feel God in moments of grace, of which a single one suffices for a lifetime. Of his own free will he disclosed himself, radiating glory, generous and gracious, full of power. And our response was a true prayer: no word from our lips, no begging, no propositions, no praise – we ourselves were a single prayer. We felt ourselves because we felt God. So mighty, so glorious is the storm of our trust that it transforms itself back into prayer ...

From the Güstrow Diary, entry for September 18, 1914. Prosa II, 61–62.

To pray, in my view, is to acknowledge the True, the indescribable Ultimate; not to beg, not to babble, not to wheedle. No, it is to comprehend this: to be consecrated – that is prayer.

Güstrow Diary, from the entry for May 7, 1915. Prosa II, 213.

If we make our God into a sort of grandfather, the dear Lord will sooner or later fail to meet the obligations we lay upon him. And then we will not believe anything any more. So – who can formulate a new concept of God for us humans, one that will not fail? How can human beings be made great enough that their faith can endure God? To lose everything, to be nothing, to have nothing, and yet to know that God is God – that would be the test. How divert man from his ever-present body and direct him towards his spirit? If I am to perish on the dunghill can I still love God? Can I, once one of the elect, still praise God and love him then? But there are worse things than perishing on the dunghill – there is guilt, and inward corrosion; there is being despoiled of all confidence and of all love, indeed of the capacity for enjoyment altogether. As long as people can have a sense of enjoyment, they are willing to be among the elect, but later, if the spark no longer kindles, if hope no longer glows, if hate and love no longer play violin duets together because their bowstrings are unstrung, then most people's concern with God is likewise over. A person no longer capable of curiosity no longer asks questions. Anyone who would like to believe actually does believe – the desire to believe is belief already. The need already betokens the fulfilment.

Güstrow Diary, from the entry for September 4, 1914. Prosa II, 42–43.

If I could bear to believe that the Almighty Spirit is ever-present and all-pervading, I should have to arrange my life differently – assuming, that is, that I am to regard the matter as of any importance whatever. I should have to let myself remain constantly all-pervaded, constantly close to God, indeed god-like, for the trifling difference would be merely external ...

But why must I spend my time toiling for bread, and for its sake tell lies and do disgraceful things? Would it not be better to go and hang myself? Yet from that the senses recoil – things would have to go far indeed before that would be the natural course to take. However, I cannot be constantly all-pervaded by God. Hence I conclude that God casts me away from him. He flings me off, as a cosmic nebula hurls its particles away into outer space, yet continues to exert a power of attraction that finally sweeps the outcast back into itself.

Güstrow Diary, Whit Monday, June 12, 1916. Prosa II, 321–322.

All in all, life's progress through changing time and space reminds me more and more of storming forward through a howling chaos, impelled by the urgent need to couple desire to destiny, with occasional breathing-spells of stillness and repose in freedom, acceptance, and deep-moved silence.

From the autobiography, A Selftold Life, 1928. Prosa I, 52.

When I lie at night and pillows of darkness press me down, sometimes a ringing light envelops me; my eyes can see it and my ears can hear. The fair forms of the better future appear there round my bed, still fixed and motionless, yet of glorious beauty; still asleep, but the one who could awaken them would give this world a better face. Whoever could do that would be a hero.

Words of the old blind wanderer Kule, from the drama The Dead Day, written 1907–1910, published 1912. Dramen, 24.

I am convinced that for me significant work was possible only after my abilities had attained separate forms of expression in both sculpture and writing. As long as I let myself be moved to creative activity by a generalized emotional urge – or more accurately, as long as I allowed anything to take form that wanted to take form – nothing but vagueness could ensue. Even now I must struggle not to let the one medium obscure the other.

I was thirty years of age when I began to express myself in the form of drama, and I feel that about this same time my feeble efforts towards plastic form began to show what I would be able to do. I do not say: what I wanted to do, for I recognized that all my conscious striving brought no return; I was forced to submit to the edict of an authority quite independent of me and my own wishes that imposed upon me a sort of inner passivity. The result is that as I write I become aware of plots and characters; my function being merely to listen to their words and to assist the course of action taken by them. Hence I can in a certain measure disclaim responsibility for them, but of course I realize that nothing comes into being except what bears some connection to my personality. In regard to this personality of mine – what I sense as limitation and narrowness, as a form of subjection, as the burdensome curse of mortality, is probably not relevant here; suffice it to say that ›I‹ am aware of myself as something other than my personality, implying that I seek my own true being in some dark unconscious depth.

Thus all my characters may well be merely fragments of this unknown darkness, emerging in order to speak and act their parts; nor do I object to the opinion that my sculptured figures are also naught but wayfarers filled with longing, pilgrims from an unknown Whence heading towards an unknown Whither.

I have to use compulsion upon myself to say even this much, and I am very conscious of my inability to give rational explanations, nor do I really see what good I accomplish by such an attempt; indeed I rather feel that all this is not my business, and that I should be content with the fact that I am aware of life and give it form as best I can.

From a letter dated Güstrow, May 10, 1926, to Edzard Schaper, then 18-year-old assistant producer at the Stuttgart Landestheater. Briefe II, 134–135.

Form – mere form? No. A mighty realisation burst upon me, and this is what it was: To you it is given to express, without reserve, all that is within you – the uttermost, the innermost, the gentle gesture of piety and the rude gesture of rage – because for everything, be it paradise, hell, or one in the guise of the other, there is expressive form.

From A Selftold Life, 1928. Prosa I, 55.

The Spirit has chosen to manifest itself in Form,
and it is not without good reason that high towers are our ideal
and that we fashion soaring beauty and upward-rearing angularity
into our symbols of Eternity

Prosa 1, 455

You told me once that the tower of St. George's in Wismar, the one with broad shoulders and thickset neck, should be called the Däubler Tower. It stands there like the transfiguration of my present worldly form, my towering, so to speak. There is indeed a reason for towers like the one at Pisa, which for all their massive weight seem like apparitions floating downward, lightly scraping their stony toes across Earth's surface, hallowing it.

Words attributed to the portly poet Theodor Däubler in the novel Seespeck, written 1913–1914, published 1948. Prosa I, 455.

On the subject of the leaning towers of Pisa: »I believe that people were weary of the eternally vertical. They wanted to try something new. And are not these towers like giant beings that float obliquely downwards from some ancient heaven, to land aslant on earth?«

Remark of Barlach's in 1915, as recounted by Friedrich Schult in Barlach im Gespräch, 1939.

Look, Martha, how the church tower seems to rise up and up, and yet of course it doesn't really rise. But in the mist its outlines are so dim that you think its steeple is trying out a little stunt up there and has vanished heavenward into thin air. I have the same good feeling that it has — for I'm quite positive that it feels good . . .

Words of Mr. Boll to his wife in the play Blue Boll, published 1926. Dramen, 394.

On one of the first days after mobilisation began, Klaus and I watched the mustering of horses for military service, on the square in front of the county courthouse . . . It was a lively and cheerful scene, everything quiet and orderly, yet ready for instant action. But over all the tossing manes, the heaving shoulders and curving haunches, the rising and falling thunder of hooves, Güstrow Cathedral's tower and nave mounted above the encompassing housetops, like music rising in architectural form, the haughty majesty of higher life above the swarming crowd, living peace amidst the restlessness. War is the turmoil of a single forenoon. And yet the tumult of the times adds its share to the fabric of eternal majesty; swarming humanity and many busy hands also created the cathedral.

From the Güstrow Diary, August 23, 1914. Published privately in part, 1943. ›Klaus‹ refers to the artist's son, born 1906. Prosa II, 24–25.

Amidst the church's heaven-storming walls and pillars, they felt their unimportance as mere human beings . . . The towering church porch of St. Mary's in Stralsund, that served as both vestibule and separate church of a supra-divine deity, inspired them more than anything else. Here all was excluded save the sense of power, of height, and of immensity. All sense of human scale was lost . . . Outside, in front of that church, only the creed of the Incomprehensible prevailed – not of the God of humankind but of non-humankind, the God of whom man has an inkling but does not include in his worship, whose service has nothing to do with the Sabbath day of rest.

From the autobiographical novel Seespeck, Prosa I, 470, 471.

. . . the chorale rose like a Titan's soul released from the church-body crystallized to stone. It spread, it freed itself, rejecting its body with a backward thrust, and rose in a rushing storm.
»Great heavens!« thought the artist, deeply moved, »God himself is there in the breast of that organist.« His searching spirit clung to the wingbeats of the chorale and swept upward in longing question . . .

From the novel Seespeck. Prosa I, 381.

. . . the world is made of suffering

Dramen, 17

(The desert. Enter the Beggar. A mob of wild children swarms about him, behaving like animals, howling like wolves. They snap at him, strike him; while they abuse him, he keeps still and patient. The Angels enter and take their stand beside him, whereupon the mob scatters.)

First Angel: In any shape we know Thee.

Second Angel: In any place we find Thee.

Beggar: There is no salvation for mankind.

(The Angels are silent.)

Beggar: My handiwork makes mock of me.

(The Angels remain silent. A sound of howling can be heard from afar.)

Beggar: That is no longer my voice; they rave in fury against me; they rage against my will. Speak!

First Angel: They do not know Thy will.

Second Angel: They do not see; they do not hear.

First Angel: Their soul knows nothing of Thee.

Beggar: Whom then does their soul know? Whom do they see, whom do they hear?

(The Angels are silent.)

Beggar: I am crushed by the weight of my wrath; I am filled with wrath against my handiwork, I am filled with wrath against myself.

(The Angels veil their faces.)

Beggar: Away with mankind, that I may find peace. Away with you likewise; back to the realms of the seraphs of light; cleanse yourselves of the reek of Earth in the glowing power of the Godhead. Leave me alone to my labors.

(Exeunt Angels. Enter the hunchback Leper.)

Leper: Howls of rage behind me, before me no ray of hope – I curse the one who brought me into this raging world... How can a world be any good if even one single soul in it is doomed to degradation? Behind me they come howling to hunt me down; they curse me, they call me wicked – and wicked I am because they hunt me down and curse me, and laugh at me and mock! And before me, what is there for me? I breathe air without hope and shall keep on breathing hopeless air until my breath stands still... Cursed is the god who made good men good and bad men bad... I'm filled with loathing of him, not of myself as I once thought, but of him who is to blame for me.

Beginning of Part II of The Flood, 1924. Dramen, 352–353.

Shall I tell you how I lost my power of sight? ... Listen – my eyes were like two spiders; they lay in wait in their hollow web and caught the images of the world that tumbled in to them; seized them and savored their delightful sweetness. But the more that came the more there were all steeped in bitterness and horror-bloated. At last my eyes could bear the sight no more; they wove the entrance over, preferred to starve within. How can I tell in words what caused the blindness of my eyes?

Kule in The Dead Day, 1912. Dramen, 23–24.

Do I not feel, deep in my heart, how the gods suffer? More than fathers, more than mothers, do they suffer. Do I not, deep in my heart, feel their joys? Greater than those of fathers, greater than those of mothers, greater than children's joys are the joys of the gods. All suffering, all joy, which they bestow on others, they know the taste of too. But the joys are far between – and the suffering of the gods is infinite.

Kule in The Dead Day, 1912. Dramen, 34.

The idea for a play occurs to me; it could be set in that amusement park in Steglitz: – a passing funeral procession and dirge, the crack of shots from a rifle-club meet, merry-go-round, roller coaster, roaring from the cages of the wild animals, all jumbled together. General mood of the Day of Judgment. Main theme: God, who stirs up this hubbub (symbol of life), how he must suffer! Because – this ferment, this dualism, this laceration of feeling, etc., – all this is an outward sign of the inner situation. Happiness, harmony – that is what is sought after, in a convulsive, wild, despairing way; disappointment, distress, and suffering – that is what is found. Urges and efforts at cross purposes within each individual betoken the troubled state of the world as a whole. Aim: – the concept of immense, of superhuman suffering, made comprehensible through human fear and pain.

Güstrow Diary, from the entry for Sunday, June 17, 1917. Concept for the play The True Sedemunds. Prosa II, 358–359.

(Interior of an Early Gothic chapel in ruinous condition ... now used as a storage room for useless odds and ends, such as old grave crosses, cracked figures carved in wood... remains of festival decorations ... In the background two slender lancet windows; offside to the right a gigantic wooden crucifix, an ancient, severely simple carving, in process of being restored, and leaning against the wall ... The oblique position makes the wooden figure of Christ appear as if about to soar upward.)

Sculptor Bromann: ... the Christus ... belongs to the very best period ... The arm I have made as replacement ... is also supposed to be of the very best period, but it has turned out in the way I learned to make it at the Academy. There is a considerable difference, I beg you to observe.

Sedemund Junior: The Christus is a masterpiece of martyrdom and anguish; the arm is that of a lazy man who has never missed a meal in his life. Pardon me for saying so! ...

Mrs. Grude: Do you know what He is saying to us? He says: Every man born of woman will some day be nailed to the Cross. Therefore guide your son in the way he should go, that when the dread hour comes he may gaze upward and soar above the world ...

Scene VI of The True Sedemunds, published 1920. The chapel resembles St. Gertrude's in Güstrow, now restored as a shrine to Barlach, who loved it dearly. Dramen, 238, 239, 240.

The Crucified, with emaciated limbs sketched in a mere half-dozen lines, would have found his hands and feet projecting over the paper's edge if this charcoal existence of his could have continued beyond those limits ...

»... his expression, his features, look as if he were suffering, not as someone can be suffering for a few hours but as if suffering were his natural condition, as if he suffered and knew no other state – and he and his cross hang there and fly through empty space, up above all creation ... I can imagine Christ hanging upon his cross, hovering in view of the earth, and compelled to suffer as long as men remain what they are. He will wait in pain until his dear Christians make up their minds to redeem him, their Redeemer, by becoming different from what they are now.«

Barlach discusses his own drawing with his son Klaus, in »The Drawing«, a word-sketch written about 1921, published 1929. Prosa II, 393, 394–395.

At this point I should like to use a word which to you, as a student of Schopenhauer, will not be without significance: the word ›Sympathy.‹ I need to feel a sense of sympathy – feel what others are feeling, suffer what they are suffering. And even where sympathy is out of place, then sympathize with myself for being so inferior, so far from resembling those who may well feel sorry for me. Sympathy need not be doleful – I can sense it equally well in my enjoyment of the heroic and the humorous. It could also be expressed as the transfer or taking over of suffering or of pleasure – that is, taking them upon myself on others' behalf. This sympathetic participation reaches the point where I find myself transported into the midst of the events visualized.

From a letter of December 28, 1911, to the publisher Reinhard Piper. Briefe II, 64–65.

I was in a desert land, full of stones and stumbling-blocks, hard for a blind man to walk in. But that was not all – that was only the least of my troubles, because the other light also, the small inner one, refused to shine any more in its secret place within me. Blackness was everywhere, not just before my eyes. Filled with a horrible fear of the dark, I heaved a heavy sigh, at which a sigh came back at me, so deep that I was shaken in spite of my own great trouble and had to say to myself: wait, there is someone else who feels twice as badly as I do. And this made me shed tears. But then from the same direction there came again such heart-rending sounds of misery that I quickly put my own troubles aside and groped my way along toward where the sobbing grew worse and worse, as if a hungry child were crying for its dead mother. And the sound came out of that big stone that you hold there in your hands. I have carried it with me ever since and have often thought to myself: better suffer in silence alone than burden others with double pain. But then at last it came clear to me, like a voice speaking in my ear: once you take upon yourself the suffering of others as well, then you become a true man.

Old Kule speaks to the Son in The Dead Day, published 1912. Dramen, 25–26.

… a sense of well-being cannot impress me, I bump my nose too soon against its walls of glass. The concept of true well-being, as it were boundless and unlimited well-being, must include freedom. But since the word ›freedom‹ can also be distorted, can even be an extorted lie, I, very personally, think that the concept also includes the Ability to Suffer, the Willingness to Suffer, so that we become resilient, constantly prepared to undertake self-renewal. To be able to throw away your selfish self means to save yourself; to be lost means to die with the power to rise again.

Güstrow Diary, from the entry for Thursday, November 5, 1914. Prosa II, 105.

To yield, to submit, to go down to defeat – is the true tragedy of failure so incomprehensible to you? Are you quite unaware that Existence itself is eternally unsatisfied? That it continually destroys itself so as to rise anew, casts itself away so as to redeem itself in a better state, keeps aspiring to the impossible only to fall short of the possible?

From an essay of 1929, posthumously published under the title a. o. »Wider den Ungeist« (»Against the False Spirit«), defending Barlach's war memorials against political interference. Prosa II, 403.

Calan: When the rats tore my eyes from their sockets, Noah, I gained true vision. I can now endure the sight of God; I behold God.
Noah (draws farther away from him).
Calan: Do you hear, Noah?
Noah: Oh Calan, what do you behold – God is my shepherd, I shall not want. He will lead me through the flood and deliver me from destruction.
Calan: That is the God of floods and of the flesh; that is the God of whom it is said that the World is tinier than nothing and God is everything. But I behold the other God, of whom it shall be said that the World is great and God is tinier than nothing – a point, a glimmer, and all things begin in him, all things end in him. He has no form and no voice.

Noah: Poor Calan!

Calan: It is you who are poor Noah! Oh Noah, how wonderful it is that God has no form and can speak no words – words that come from the flesh. God is only a glow, a glimmering spark; all things pour forth from him and all things return again to the fathomless depths of his glow. He creates and is himself created anew by that which he has created.

Noah: Oh Calan – God, who changeth not from everlasting unto everlasting?

Calan: I too; I too am about to return to the source from which I was cast forth; God will be augmented by me, and with me will transform himself anew. How wonderful it is, Noah, that I too am no longer a form but only a glow and a fathomless depth in God – I am sinking into him now; already he is transformed into me and I into him – he with my baseness, I with his majesty – one single One.

From the final scene of The Flood, 1924, where the powerful pagan Calan has been bound by the sons of Noah and left outside the Ark to perish in the approaching Flood. Dramen, 382–383.

... Death in all these forms became his life's companion ...

Prosa II, 453

Elise: I took you by the hand, in the stream of refugees ... no breath remains within me for kind words ... here, we are at the place from whence all Grace has fled. Let us get away, help us.

Thomas: Away, away, away from here ...

Klinkerfuss: And what about Death and the Devil, Thomas – what about Kasper, all these puppets of ours – and me, your old father?

From the miracle play The Foundling, 1922, close in time and theme to this woodcut. Dramen, 282.

(In the background the ›Chorus of Vengeance‹ sings a parody of the Wedding March from Lohengrin) ...

Iver (who has been standing opposite Fräulein Isenbarn): How did you get into this kind of a place?

Frl. Isenbarn: How? I do not know how, I am just here.

Iver: But do you fit in here, then?

Frl. Isenbarn: Well, do you?

Iver: Good Lord, when I think of some of the places I've gone dancing in – they couldn't always be first class. However, things are going to be different; I intend to get out of here – will you come with me? ... You and I must come from the same part of the world, we speak the same language ... But ssh! nobody is to know it, for that region stands in poor repute in some people's opinion – they could make remarks. I am going straight home ... but you probably have to dance around once more, so good-bye – have fun!

Dialogue from the play The Poor Cousin, written 1911–1913, published 1918. Typical Burlach ›double-talk‹, as the region referred to by the hero is the ›other world‹ and he is about to die. Dramen, 150–151.

I feel as if I had died too, and had shaken off everything just as he has done ... At last my turn has come ... at last I am satisfied with myself. I can sense a new beginning, at long last a beginning! Must a person go to his grave, to get away from it all? No, Beginning and Ending can be combined and linked together. You may mock at his ending ... but just you leave the Beginning alone ... it is my property, this Beginning of which I can be conscious both when I'm awake and asleep, like an infant newly born. We may not know right from left yet be in the midst of everything, immersed in the Newness that seems so perfectly natural. But now we must learn to see, to creep, to walk, and in due course all the rest. And good Lord, just think what all that can be!

Fräulein Isenbarn renounces the materialistic way of life, in the play The Poor Cousin, 1918. Dramen, 178, 181.

»Yes«, he thought, »how strange it was ... in those days one knew nothing, but imagined and felt everything; in those days there were ghosts behind every object and you moved past softly, half fearful, half curious, and dared not cast a glance backward. Faint inner music hinted at a Life that might be everywhere, in everything.« The old home of his childhood had called to him in a whisper of infinite tenderness out of the far distant past, but the gentle tremor was enough to open his heart and pour forth its modest souvenirs – memories fraught with painful pleasure, as when in our dreams we behold those dead and gone, arise once more before our shaken soul. »If only we could have a faith«, the thought occurred to him, »even a superstition, something to which we could cling with the same sort of bliss as in childhood.«

From the autobiographical novel Seespeck, written 1913–1914, published 1948. Prosa I, 357.

... Wau was haunted at this period by the swarm of sombre thoughts which assailed him from time to time ever since his boyhood days. Before his mind's eye there passed, not as apparitions but as actual presences which he had no wish to avoid, the array of his dead ancestors and relatives, as he had known them during their lifetime, had followed the course of their existence, and had shared the experience of their demise, at least to the extent of being completely familiar with all the details thereof. Each of them had had a hard death. For all of them Death had come with ruthless violence, or at the very least with callous cruelty, to execute the pitiless verdict from the soundless lips of the Judge.

The deep stir of Wau's emotion whenever he experienced anew with memory's eye the death of one or other of those near and dear to him – his father, his mother, his brothers and others – overwhelmed him for days at a time ... so that Death in all these implacable forms eventually became his life companion, and he had long since dismissed from his mind the possibility that his own decease might some day be a more peaceful passing than had that of the others.

From the final autobiographical novel, The Stolen Moon, written 1936–1937, just before Barlach's own hard death. Published 1948. Prosa II, 453.

The grave is for me a gruesome place, I must confess; all the philosophy I take such pains to hammer together collapses at times like a house of cards (not only at the actual ›grave‹ either) and then I'm attacked once again by harassing »Why«s and »Wherefore«s, unmuzzled and with hellish sharpened teeth.

The gruesomeness of the whole performance is the part we can be sure of, a bitter burden the mind must bear; as to whether it all has a meaning, a purpose – we may piously assume this to be the case, yet we do not know for certain, and under this curse we writhe our way through the years and so into the grave. The wretched final stage of decrepitude and decay, of late so constantly before my eyes, fills me with embittered loathing. What a botched-up job – do you wonder that I turn orthodox and that I can symbolize this existence of ours as nothing but penitentiary, banishment, hell, degradation, etc.? – And yet I am really determined to keep cheerful in the face of it all, so as to keep alive my hope for the possible existence, somewhere or other, of a world of peace.

From a letter to Reinhard Piper, dated June 1, 1921, just after the suicide of Barlach's mother. Briefe II, 105–106.

The beckoning finger of a friendly hand pointed out to the tormented girl the peaceful well-being on the face of the poor dead pauper – Old Friend Death went quietly with her down the stairs; and on their homeward way the sobs of this dear young charge of his mingled with the sighs of sympathetic Night ... Silent and solicitous, he brought her into the home of self-oblivion, and with a deep sigh of bliss she realised that the place to which she was led was the final and finest refuge for her in this world, and that the one who led her thither was bringing her home like a bride to her resting-place free from all care.

Death of Frieda Wunderlich in The Stolen Moon, written 1936–1937, published 1948. Prosa II, 653.

I should like to work up a play, something to this effect: the dead are not dead, but we cannot endure the idea that they exist and know all about us. We reject them; we have to forget in order to be able to live our own life. We shudder at the thought that they might be around us, watching everything we do. In the final analysis, God – who sees, knows, and remembers all things – well, it is the same with God as with the dead. We cannot endure him, and it finally amounts to this: nobody believes in God since nobody behaves as if God were ever-present. We can produce wonderful controversial statements about him, such as: "God does not exist, just as the dead do not exist, i. e. not for us, not for our senses, not for our reason." "God has been appointed by the wealthy as a bailiff, a policeman. It is they themselves who go round spying, but they claim it is God who does." "Whoever really believed in God would have to die, assuming that he is in earnest and not merely disguising a human form as the deity (deifying it)."

It is actually in gods that we believe, since each of us has in his soul the image of 'his' God. We cannot endure that a single dead person should continue to exist and know everything, so how much less an all-mighty, all-knowing God. Then what? We do want a God. Well, then we must construct one. If I tell a lie, just once, God knows it, and even if he forgives it, he cannot forget it. Neither can I, and when I come before God, my lie comes with me into Eternity. Consequently: since God does exist, he must be different from us, namely without recollection, without knowledge, without judgment. This I cannot know for certain; I can neither hear it nor see it, hence I cannot absolutely believe it. But I must have something that I am able to believe, that is certain. Joy, desire, compulsion, volition – that is God.

Güstrow Diary, from the entry for February 28, 1916; ideas for the drama The True Sedemunds. Prosa II, 314–315.

We both love God very much, Awah. I know more about him than my father Noah and all the others do ... God is not everywhere, and God is not in everything, the way my father Noah says. He conceals himself behind all things and in all things there are narrow openings, fine slits that he shines through, shines and flashes. Thin, narrow slits, so fine that you never find them again if you turn your head away for a moment ... I often see him through these slits, but it all takes place so strangely fast – one moment they spring open and then the next moment close without trace of a join – strange, Awah.

Noah's son Shem talks to the pagan maiden Awah, in the play The Flood, published 1924. Dramen, 354–355.

(Grude and his wife come forward arm in arm. Suddenly he takes hold of her and dances along for part of the way.)
Mrs. Grude: Don't dear! Walk quietly now and save your dancing till later. Wait until we get away from these graves first.
Grude: Ah no – it's the graves I want to dance across; it's this creepiness I want to cut right through, tread it down into the crypt! The old folks have had their day and are laid low under the sod; the day now belongs to us and to our children after us. Everything will be changed from the ground up – hurrah for the new day and hurrah for the true Grudes!

Final scene of The True Sedemunds, published 1920. Dramen, 265.

Inordinate Greed destroys too much of our human kindliness,
spawning a breed that is filled with lowbred instincts;
this breed takes for its god not an ennobled "Ego"
but a gluttonous bestial "Ego" to whose service it devotes
all its gifts of body, mind, and spirit

From a letter to brother Hans Barlach, June 6, 1922. Briefe II, 110

God of Gluttony, Lord of my hollow stomach
Grant layers of fat upon my scrawny frame;
Thy will be that I live a lusty life in heaven and on earth;
Lead us into temptation with good drinks
And deliver us from indigestion;
For thine is the kingdom, the power, and the glory of everlasting Gluttony
In the Devil's name.

Prayer of a starving man in The Foundling, written 1920, published 1922. Dramen, 278–279.

This Earth is poor stuff for Thy working, there lies wolfseed within it. Earths permeates Man with her essence, she nurses him with wolfish milk. What children suck from their mother's breast bursts forth in burning fury from their eyes... Unto beasts and images of clay they build their temples, and to these ghastly gods they grant the majesty of Thy greatness... Thy world has fallen into frenzy.

The Angels address God in the drama The Flood, 1924. Dramen, 335–336.

Everything is being smothered in flesh.

A leitmotif of the drama Blue Boll, 1926. Dramen, 396.

Cut out all that meat, she often says to the children; bacon and ham and sausage, she says, will make you into bacon and sausage. Are you nothing but stomachs, or what?... Getting fattened up is all right for the livestock, it's a point of honor for pigs, but are children pigs? Cut out the meat, do away with the flesh, she says; the Pastor is quite right, he says so too – that was when she had just come from church.

Cited words of Greta Gruental, wife of the swineherd in the play Blue Boll, 1926. Dramen, 388.

Our ruler, the Red Kaiser, thus makes proclamation:
That daily we all face the accusation
That Man eats Man, that we devour our brothers,
That all of us live by pursuit of others.
Our ruler, the Red Kaiser, thus proclaims:
Wicked it is to dare eat human flesh,
Wicked it is to savor human blood,
But worse, with ill will aimed against our brothers,
To gnaw upon the hearts and minds of others,
With love torment, through hate degrade,
Refusing favor and denying aid.

Words of a messenger in The Foundling, modern miracle play, 1922. Dramen, 272.

People believe only in the happiness of Having; they must also learn to believe in the happiness of Giving. Giving grants Grace. The gift of one's self, the greatest Grace. Man is constituted thus: he yearns passionately for something he can possess – a property, a faith, an altar on which he can offer himself completely. Therefore: give man a goal with real meaning and he will hurl himself towards Grace and Happiness and reckon not the cost. But where there is no meaning, no supra-personal goal, everything is poured into the belly and the moneybag.

Words of Sedemund Junior in the play The True Sedemunds, published 1920. Dramen, 200.

The baker ... rocked back and forth, his hands folded across his belly ... and then settled back into the low-slung balance of his massive flesh. He may well have been asleep, even though his pig-eyes continued to peer vacantly into the light ... "How's this?" thought Seespeck, "is this great clod of a baker a condemned soul who here, before our very eyes, has put on a demonstration of his torture and his guilt? Is this mass of corporeal uncleanliness actually conscious of its own unclean spirituality? What a potentate of Evil!"

From the novel Seespeck. Prosa I, 344.

'My' God – that is what it amounts to, too – he is my concept, the idealized image in my own mirror. And yet – Universal Spirit? One comprising all things? Hence even all qualities of roguery and rottenness? Would "rogue and rotter" then merely exist in my own mind? Actually be just another kind of refraction of the spirit?

Güstrow Diary, from entry for June 12, 1916. Prosa II, 320.

If God is all things, where does that leave the wicked?

Words of Calan, Noah's antagonist, in The Flood. Dramen, 352.

Calan, God's enemy ... says that Good comes from God's goodness and Evil from God's badness – if God were only good and nothing but good, then God's badness would not be evil, and all Evil would be Good ...

Words of Noah, somewhat shaken by Calan's argument, in The Flood, 1924. Dramen, 361.

Devil and God are one. Thus One is Two. Are end and means two? Happiness is not a final end, tranquillity is not a final end, yet there has to be the surge of struggle to attain happiness, tranquillity. Happiness and tranquillity must include tribulation and turbulence. Or in other words: double-nature, thousand-sidedness, is the end achieved by the great Unity. In order to be One, there must be infinite Multiplicity. Unity does not exist without diversity ... Happiness does not exist without tribulation, nor salvation without sin. Eternal harmony requires eternal dissonance. Night is the soul of day, day the creator of night. Love must exist, but it would be a mere phantom without mutual sympathy, without the feeling: we belong together because we do not belong to the others. Without hate no love. Eternal bliss requires eternal pain in order to glow and blaze, it is kindled and fed thereupon. Bliss is the true and the pure, but not without lie and error. Because we are lost, therefore we can be saved. In order that the soul may be able to live, the body must be able to die. Height is naught without depth. Thus One does exist! All is One. Yet in order that it may perceive itself as One it must be infinite. In order that I may perceive, I must be able to differentiate. In order that All-One may exist, all must be different. God and Devil may not be reconciled. Devil as Depth, God as Height, together Depth and Height create a Whole.

From »The Day of Judgment«, part of a section in diary notes headed »Theodor Däubler«, written about 1914, published posthumously 1959. Prosa II, 380.

. . . to make forms emerge out of the mystery of Existence . . .

Barlach in a conversation, 1932

He had limbs that seemed carved out of the cliff on which he stood; the stubborn, massive forms reared steeply upward, as if piled there by some giant hand to build a towering wall against the sea; firm and unshaken they had stood there through the centuries, and in their features was revealed, in spite of yawning clefts and deep-cut cracks, a will of granite to continue thus throughout the centuries to come.

From the word-sketch »The Lifeguard«, undated but probably before 1900; first published 1939. Prosa I, 225.

... and Seespeck saw a head reminiscent of Martin Luther, peasant-like, with rough-hewn features, set on a body not actually fat but rather looking as if it were chopped out with an axe from a sturdy block.

Description of Barlach's friend Dr. Klencke from the novel Seespeck. Prosa I, 450.

(His shoulder) had grown crooked from carrying great loads; by its very nature it was designed to break things up, to make them burst, to overthrow all that stands firm and to move all that stands still.

Desciption of the mysterious, powerful Red Kaiser in the modern miracle play The Foundling, 1922. Dramen, 298.

Growth and emergent form can follow curious courses ... You cannot even spit without hitting a spot where something lies waiting to be brought to life, all ready to crack its cocoon ... Become your own true self, that's the thing!

Words of the informal, anonymous »gentleman« inferred to be God in the play Blue Boll, 1926. Dramen, 417.

All this craving for the spiritual, this desire and search for God, does have meaning. It is, to put it roughly, to merge oneself with God, that is: to comprehend God, to feel as he does, to share his exalted state, to ›behold‹ him, be this simply in the sense of grasping the real meaning of the world, of human existence.

Güstrow Diary, from the entry for June 12, 1916 (Whit Monday). Prosa II, 321.

Christopher: Venture with me along this same way; it is a way of service without lord or master above you or below ...
Heinrich: It is well, friend Christopher; go now and seek out the lord and master whom you most desire; seek, serve and then spurn him for the sake of a still greater lordliness; and be you in your search your own lord and master, sensing the lordliness of the highest lord within your own soul. I was your first lord, you yourself will not be your own ultimate lord, for there will always be one beyond ...
Christopher: ... the supreme joy is the uniting of obedience with its opposite, the union of self-gaining with self-giving ... Of such kind is my obedience, for thus I am both servant and master ... (he prays) God, thou who didst grant that I should feel this joy, thine be the praise and the thankfulness of my soul, in the joy of obedience, in harmony with lordliness of self ... Praise God as I do, and unite with me in God's praise.
Heinrich: I have no God – but praise be that this is how is is: I do not have a God but God has me.

Final wisdom from the last scene of the last play, The Count of Ratzeburg, completed by 1927, published 1950. Dramen, 571–572, 571.

They try to classify me according to my philosophy of life – they call me a ›God-seeker‹. But a God-seeker, what does that mean, actually? I would consider it out-and-out arrogance if someone else made that claim for himself. They stick the labels ›cultist‹ and ›mystic‹ on my works, and rack their brains trying to find riddles in what I present, and then infer that I artfully make their solution difficult. Yet I desire nothing whatever but to be an artist pure and simple. It is my belief that that which cannot be expressed in words can be conveyed to others through Form. It satisfies both my personal desire and my creative urge to hover and to circle again and again over the problems of the meaning of Life and other grand mountain peaks in the realm of the spirit. There I can always find plenty of material to ruminate over until I wear down the teeth of my mind. – But to preach, to present solutions, to assign values, to define Good and Evil – in a word, to do anything whatsoever except make forms emerge out of the mystery of Existence, forms which are credible and which acquire only as much of me as I am permitted to give them – this shall not be allowed to creep into my art.

From a conversation reported by Georg Gretor in the newspaper Politiken, Copenhagen, on July 8, 1932. Translated direct from the Danish original.

... as far as I am concerned, organic structure in nature is the outer expression of the inner essence; the human form is the expression of God, to whatever extent he can be sensed within man and behind man, brooding and probing. Can the inner essence be expressed by abstract lines? By anything save the visible exterior? Can anything except expression be used for expressing something? ... Can we depict the wheels and mechanism of a clock and say: »This is the time«, instead of showing the sun's equivalent in the form of the dial-plate and the movement of the hands of the clock? To render the psyche in tangible form one must make joy, pain, sympathy, hope, and despair visible – and in what better manner than on the dial-plate of the human face by means of the clock-hand pattern of its lines and wrinkles? ... And, finally, it is the human eye, ear, senses, that are to be satisfied and stimulated, and I am unable to shape a world that does not exist; I have to express myself by means of intelligible signs.

From the notebook musings of 1912–1914, called by Barlach »Diario Däubler«, first published 1959. Prosa II, 374, 375.

Apparent truths pass away, Truth itself remains, wordless, a tempest tossing formal dogmas to and fro, exposing time-honored fallacies; a living force that lends the transitory substance of these dogmas the strength to flourish until, over-ripe, they rot away. Individual truths are sensate and man-made, Truth is the essence of invisibility, the Being of being, the unnamable for which our monosyllabic sound merely serves as a sign that human imperfection is conscious of the perfection of the Superhuman, to which it gives a name simply in order to label it as something existent: the emanation of the eternally unknown God, something not of human scale hence not comprehensible to humans, accordingly unknown to them now and forever.

The artist's type of belief, however, not overburdened with logic, trusts in its own creative force, and proves at least to his satisfaction that he has a part to play in the grand creative course of existence.

From »Poet's Credo«, an essay published in Voices of Religious Experience, 1931. Prosa II, 408.

...my work as a Whole is in a good state...

Briefe II, 220

A powerful radiant warmth, from the direction of heaven, is at work.

Towards the end of the play Blue Boll, 1926. Dramen, 452.

Being alive is an everyday business, but coming to life is strange and wonderful, eh, Klaus?

Barlach thinks of his eight-year-old son as he writes his diary for September 25, 1914. Güstrow Diary, Prosa II, 68.

To sit quietly like that in the evening, beside the stove in Sønderborg, for an hour or perhaps two, sometimes for only half an hour – that was a great experience. The experience of one's own self. I discovered myself – nothing special, nothing elegant or beautiful or distinguished or clever or admirable, no – only my Self: whatever it is that is Real about me. The Real is the opposite of ›Reality‹. I wrote to Mrs. Mendelssohn-Bartholdy in the evening, as I sat smoking my cigar, that I felt like someone who has fallen down a steep slope and then regains consciousness and gradually begins to sense that all his limbs are intact and that after all he is quite comfortable lying there. Astonishment, peace, pleasure in the unthinking perception of Time. Not as in sleep, rather as in a heightened sense of watchful consciousness, but without any shape to one's thoughts. In the same way as an infant stares out into the world, absorbing form and color and knowing nothing save wonder, feeling nothing save satisfaction at all this wonder. The Newness is the wonder, in my opinion – this look into the unknown. My Self has begun something like new existence in the world.

Güstrow Diary, from the entry for February 28, 1916, just after returning from eight weeks military training in Slesvig, then part of Germany. Prosa II, 313–314.

Good Lord, yes indeed, a sense of gladness is the truest form of piety, I do believe. And I think I can claim for myself that in the final analysis I am thankful and trusting. Trusting – in what? – in the Whole, in the Universal, in the mystery of existence. My Creator Father may well look with little favor upon me but nevertheless I thank him from the depths of my being. Whatever the answer to the riddle turns out to be, it must be accepted.

Güstrow Diary, from the entry for Sunday, December 17, 1916. Prosa II, 346.

Even at an advanced age he was not a senile old man – sometimes he seemed young, sometimes old, depending on the mood of the moment... I am not certain that I ever did see his true form, probably not – I have only seen some of his transformations. But there is one of his phases I should like to recall as perhaps being closest to his true form: that of a tired old gentleman, sprinkled ever so slightly with the dust of want and worry, yet enjoying a moment of mild good cheer in a quiet nook somewhere, away from the unceasing baying clamor going on outside.

Description of friend Albert Kollmann, in a memorial essay first published 1921. Prosa II, 391–392.

If that is the way you want it, Mr. Boll, I'll not lift the cloak of anonymity which you have put upon me, or at most just a trifle and incidentally, as a sign of intimacy between the two of us. Yes, Mr. Boll, ›Lord God‹ is what you have been calling me – well, between ourselves, there is something in it, but only in the sense of a modest, gentle reflection from Infinity will I consent to accept the title of God, a faint, almost imperceptible, shading of divinity – that is what you mean, is it not?

Words of the character in Blue Boll called simply »Herr«, which may mean either »gentleman« or »Lord«. Dramen, 426.

The role of »Herr« is indeed a very, very tricky one; in my opinion it cannot be played informally enough, indeed I believe that the more his activity in the play appears commonplace, so to speak philistine, seemingly unimportant and inconsequential, the greater will be the effectiveness of the sense of fate that is conceived as a dark force, sovereign and creative, in the background of all that happens. Anything this incomprehensible can only be accepted as a matter of course, like the rising and setting of the sun.

From a letter to Edzard Schaper, published under the title »Barlach über sein Schaffen und Sein« in Schwäbische Thalia, 1926, 42–44.

Man is still evolving, he has not become anything yet ... Our personal existence ... is only a wellspring, but Life a great River of continual Growth, with no goal save further fulfilment – eternal Becoming! Today is but its feeble dawning, tomorrow will be outshone by the day after.

Cited »message« in the play Blue Boll, 1926. Dramen, 400.

The outlook is good, since you are a man of solid substance and you have the strength to strive – for suffering and struggle, my dear sir, are the implements of Growth ... Growth fulfits itself timelessly, our lifetime is but its dim semblance. Ponder all this in your heart, let it be sufficient unto the day.

Final words of the »Herr« to Mr. Boll. Dramen, 455.

The fact that I achieved a calm and cheerful state of mind during my work on the six figures (three were finished earlier) makes me especially grateful to them ... I once remarked to you that there is a law that no work can turn out successfully unless it goes through a severe crisis that deepens and spiritualizes it ... On that count my work as a whole is in a good state; in that respect it can stand scrutiny.

From a letter to cousin Karl Barlach in the time of trouble and oppression, referring to the nine sculptured figures of the Frieze of the Listeners, Reemtsma Collection, Hamburg. December 12, 1935. Briefe II, 220.

I am well over sixty now, and begin to achieve a fuller understanding of life ... I conceive of life as a never-ending process, the strength of whose rhythmic heartbeat has weakened little if at all and remains my deepest, most secret joy. Within this pattern, all my earlier efforts can be looked upon as formative phases, each of which I passed through in sincere conviction, none of which I can consider my final or utmost ... I have nothing to recant but much to fulfil – considering fulfilment as the ultimate realisation of all my abilities in complete coordination. What makes me happy is the absolute naturalness with which all this takes place.

From a letter to Alfred Heuer, dated Güstrow, November 11, 1932. Briefe I, 76.

... in the book in which my hand has written the name of God ten times on every page, the shepherd says: »I am ashamed to speak of God ... the word is too big for my mouth. I comprehend that he is not to be comprehended – that is all my knowledge of him.« Well, my own comprehending is like that of the shepherd; into the torrent of words about God he drops a small word for me personally. It is best not to talk about it ... Anyway, I consider that each individual is entitled to adapt the concept of the Highest to suit himself. Just as I do too.

From a letter to Dore Schultz-Reutti, dated July 28, 1929, referring to The Flood. Briefe II, 149.

From time to time I resolve not to use the word »God« any more, because I am crushed by the consciousness of the discrepancy between the amount we mortals are able to sense and comprehend, and the concept which includes All-Being and All-Happening ... Unfortunately I am an artist and compelled by my natural disposition to perceive form in all things. And in a general analogous way, God has ›become‹ what he is because of human and artistic inability to grasp the formless and boundless. Because, in a word, whether he wants to or not, Man must create Form.

From a letter dated Güstrow, December 3, 1932, to Pastor Johannes Schwartzkopff. Briefe II, 182.

Thou from everlasting unto everlasting
Thou Beginning without Ending
Thou Glory, Thou Holiness
Greatness, Goodness
Storm and Stillness
All-Seeing and All-Being

The seven woodcuts republished here were originally issued as Die Wandlungen Gottes / Sieben Holzschnitte von Ernst Barlach, in the Pan Press of Paul Cassirer, Berlin, 1922, in two editions:

A. Deluxe edition of 121 copies numbered I–XI and 1–110; each woodcut printed by hand and signed by the artist; the individual prints measuring between 250 and 257 millimetres ($9^7/8$ and $10^1/8$ inches) in height, and 358–360 millimetres ($14^1/8$–$14^3/16$ inches) in width. Bound in parchment.

B. Popular edition machine-printed by galvanotype from the original woodblocks by the firm of Wilhelm Wagner, 1922. Bound in grey cardboard.

All the original woodblocks, with the exception of that for »The First Day«, were destroyed during Barlach's lifetime.

The set of seven was reprinted by Christian Kaiser, Munich, 1954, in a popular edition, the prints being reproduced by offset technique in slightly reduced size.

The present publication is made with the kind permission of Mr. Nikolaus Barlach and owes its appearance – in both senses – to the unfailing encouragement and support of the Ernst Barlach Gesellschaft e. V., especially of Professor Hans Harmsen, Chairman, and Dr. Wolf Stubbe, Archivist, both of Hamburg, as well as to the generous sponsorship of internationally-minded authorities in the Foreign Office of the West German government – to all of whom sincere gratitude is herewith expressed.

Principal source of the seventy-four selections translated is the definitive edition of Barlachs writings, published by R. Piper & Co., Munich – Ernst Barlach: Das dichterische Werk in drei Bänden / I. Die Dramen, 1956; II. Die Prosa I, 1958; III. Die Prosa II, 1959. In addition: Ernst Barlach, Aus seinen Briefen (»Briefe I«), Piper, Munich, 1947; Ernst Barlach: Leben und Werk in seinen Briefen (»Briefe II«), Piper, Munich, 1952; Barlach im Gespräch, collected and printed by Friedrich Schult, Güstrow, 1939; the periodical Schwäbische Thalia; and the newspaper Politiken, Copenhagen.

Umschlag: Kurt August, Klischees: Willi Uhrmacher, Satz und Druck: Hans Christians Druckerei, Einband: Buchbinderei Richard Naumann, alle in Hamburg.